The Environment

The Insider Career Guides is a dynamic series of books designed to give you the inside track on individual careers – how to get in, how to get on, even how to get out.

Based on the real-life experiences of people actually working in these fields, each title offers a combination of hard practical information and insider information on working culture, the pros and cons of different areas of work, prospects for promotion, etc.

Other titles in the series:

Banking and the City
Karen Holmes

Information and Communications Technology
Jacquetta Megarry

Retailing
Liz Edwards

Sport
Robin Hardwick

Travel and Tourism
Karen France

About the Series Editor
Following a successful career as a teacher and lecturer in the UK and the Far East, Karen Holmes now works as a freelance writer, editor and project manager. Specialising in learning and careers, she has authored a range of careers literature for publishers and other commercial organisations.

The Environment

by

Melanie Allen

First published in 1999 by
The Industrial Society
Robert Hyde House
48 Bryanston Square
London W1H 7LN

© The Industrial Society 1999

ISBN 1 85835 588 5

British Library Cataloguing-in-Publication Data.
A catalogue record for this book is available from the
British Library.

Typeset by: The Midlands Book Typesetting Company
Printed by: Cromwell Press
Cover by: Sign Design
Cover image by: Paul Vozdic/Photonica

The Industrial Society is a Registered Charity No. 290003

CONTENTS

the environment

INTRODUCTION

How do you find out about a career that interests you? You contact organisations that work in the relevant industry, look at recruitment literature and talk to the professionals, the people who already work there. That is just what we have done to prepare this series of books.

Based on real-life experiences and information from industry employees, *The Insider Career Guides* give you the inside story on what it is really like to work in a particular field of employment. These titles will help you find out more about different professions and their cultures, the day-to-day working routines and the opportunities that exist.

In this book, *The Insider Career Guide to the Environment*, you will find a useful overview of:

- the kinds of jobs that may be open to you
- what the work is like in a range of jobs
- how to make a start in your chosen career
- the qualities employers are looking for in their new recruits
- the pay and benefits you can expect
- opportunities for training and development
- promotion, and the way to the top.

This book is divided into three sections:

Part One, *The Job*, gives you an overview of the environment industry, including:

- background and current trends in a new and changing industry
- brief descriptions of some of the areas of employment within the environment sector

- an insight into the jobs of some of the people already working in the industry
- the terms and conditions that generally apply.

Part Two, *The Person*, focuses on the people who work in the industry. Starting with a questionnaire to help you assess your own personal qualities and skills which would help you survive and thrive in the world of environmental work, it goes on to look at:

- the skills and experience you are likely to need for a job in the environment sector
- the personal characteristics that will help you in the job
- inside information from people who work in the industry about their working lifes.

Part Three, *Getting in, Getting on. . . Getting out*, looks at:

- where you can find out about current vacancies
- how to make applications that catch the eye of recruiters
- the training and development you are likely to receive once you join
- opportunities for promotion and advancement
- related careers – where do people who leave the industry go next?

No book can tell you everything you want to know. *The Insider Career Guide to the Environment* can only offer information on some of the jobs and career opportunities in the environment industry – an industry difficult to pin down and define. You will probably want to do your own research. Useful contact and website addresses are provided in *Want to find out more?* on page 67, so that you can get the additional information you need.

In this book, there are case histories, quotes from industry workers and 'myth busters' which address popular misconceptions about working for and in the environment. You'll find plenty of inside information in these pages to see whether a job or a career in the environment is for you, to give you a flavour of what may be available and to point you in the right direction.

As we researched this area, we began to realise how diverse the industry and the job-market really was. The resulting case histories outlined in Part One can only offer a broad idea of what it might be like for you, and the kind of opportunities that exist at the time of writing. There is no typical job, no typical career path and no typical organisation. Jobs, employers, career paths, salaries and conditions all vary considerably.

This book will help anyone thinking of a career in the environment – whether you are a school leaver, a graduate or if you want to move from a job you already have. There is a great deal of competition for work in this industry. Although new and different opportunities are opening up by the minute, there continues to be a greater number of people competing for jobs than there are jobs available. Consequently, you would be well advised to think about entering as a graduate, preferably in a science, geography or geology – even if you want a job that does not specifically require you to have a degree.

part one   the job

the job

Introduction

If you see yourself as an eco-warrior, fighting to save the world, put this book down now. Jobs on the Rainbow Warrior are not really up for grabs, and you might as well forget glamour, idealism and adventure. That is not to say that the jobs available are necessarily unsatisfying, humdrum or boring. What it does mean is that you need to be pragmatic and realistic about your role as an environmentalist, and about the opportunities that could be available to you.

A keen interest in the environment is obviously important, as many of the jobs you are likely to be looking at will not, as a rule, be very well paid. One comment from a finance manager working in a not-for-profit agency was, 'Don't expect to make any money!' This advice was echoed by many other people we interviewed. On the plus side, almost everyone enjoyed their work, and many of them had taken a drop in salary to be able to move sideways and enter the industry – with no regrets. The level of commitment and enthusiasm of industry employees was refreshing.

⌐ MYTH BUSTER ⌐

Work in the environment is all about fighting to make the world a better place

Not altogether true – many jobs in the environment sector are about limiting the damage that people do, working within the constraints of environmental regulations. Yes, you will be contributing to making the world a better place, but achievement is on a small scale, and is often hard-won.

'Most of my job is about policing and enforcing regulations for water pollution – if I manage to solve a small problem with a septic tank, I feel I have achieved something.'

Environment protection officer

In this section, the focus is on some of the work available in this country, and the kind of work or career opportunities available to anyone who is interested in working in the environment industry. We look at overall working conditions, organisational culture and conventions, and more specifically at working in:

- the voluntary sector: charities and trusts
- local authorities
- agencies or non-departmental public bodies (NDPBs) – not-for-profit organisations funded by the Government, set up to manage and enforce Government policies and regulations.

These are the areas where most opportunities are currently available, and where most of the change and growth in the industry will probably manifest itself in the future.

Jobs are also available in the private sector, as more of the larger organisations employ environmental professionals in-house. Consultancies are becoming more of a feature of the market, acting in an advisory capacity, and waste collection, waste disposal, landfill and recycling are areas where profits can be made.

Central Government (the Department of the Environment, Transport and the Regions – DETR) also offers a number of career opportunities.

Growth and change in the industry

Environmental issues have become more and more a part of everyday life and work in recent years. Paper recycling, bottle banks and a general awareness of the harm we humans do to the environment are part of the received wisdom of our lives. Similarly, environmentalists used to be a minority group, viewed with suspicion and associated with vegetarianism, strange shoes and earnest oddball puritanism. Things have changed. Most of us are aware of our environments, vegetarians are not considered to be cranks, bottles 'to go to the bottle bank' litter people's houses, and a good summer invariably provokes discussion about global warming.

Ten years ago, this book would have been very different. There would have been more about rural issues, wildlife and hedgerows and very little about urban renewal, local environments and community involvement. Environmental issues have entered the mainstream and consequently the job market is gathering pace. That means that scope and number of associated jobs and careers is increasing. All of which looks promising from your point of view as a potential recruit in the industry. However, you need to bear in mind that though this is true, young people are also more interested in being a part of the industry. Competition is fierce.

MYTH BUSTER

Jobs in the environment are about working in the country – trees, ponds and the conservation of species of flowers and wildlife

Well – some still are, but by far the majority of environmental work goes on in urban areas. And with the Government's regeneration and New Deal for Community drives, this trend is likely to continue.

'It took me a whole year to understand that my job wasn't about mending fences, but about people and their involvement in the environment they live in.'

Project officer in a trust committed to improving the environment

What people say about their work in the environment

Jobs, careers and career paths are all different, as has been said before, so it is difficult to generalise about the actual work that is done in the environment industry. However, one or two recurring themes have emerged in the course of our research.

The first is that almost everyone we spoke to enjoyed their work and were committed to caring for the environment, from environment protection officers to people who worked in the PR or finance departments, and volunteer rangers.

When asked what the key skills and qualities for the work might be, excluding formal qualifications, everyone we interviewed flagged up communication, people skills and flexibility of approach. Most of the jobs in this area involve working with people and being able to communicate clearly, whether you are inspecting an abattoir, negotiating with other professionals or taking local schoolchildren on an outing to a farm. Flexibility is important as most jobs involve a variety of activities, and you need to be able to use your initiative and discretion and adapt to the changing needs of your role.

Even a countryside ranger, romantically seen as the rugged individualist at one with nature, with no time for the human race, has to be able to educate, communicate with the public diplomatically and liaise with other people. Litter picking, mending fences and ponds, organising activities with conservation groups, giving talks to raise awareness of conservation issues and working with community work groups are all duties you would be expected to perform as a ranger. Although this is the job most often associated with environmental work, we have not featured it as one of the profiles that follow, as there are currently only just over 1,000 permanent positions available in the UK.

When the interviewees were asked whether there was anything they disliked about their jobs, most of them (but not all) mentioned paperwork – writing reports, keeping other people informed of what they were doing, filling in forms and writing bids for funding.

WORKING IN AN ENVIRONMENTAL AGENCY

There is a wide spread of jobs and careers concerned with the environment available in the various environmental agencies or non-departmental public bodies (formerly called quangos, before the word was discredited!). The Environment Agency for England and Wales and the Scottish Environment Protection Agency (SEPA) are examples of these.

The Environment Agency (England and Wales) was established in April 1996 from the merging of the National Rivers Authority, Her Majesty's Protection of Pollution and the Local Waste Regulation Authorities. The Agency is responsible for the protection and management of the environment in England and Wales by combining the regulation of land, air and water. Its remit covers nature conservation, flood defence, fisheries and pollution prevention and control, among other things. It is structured into seven regions in England and one in Wales, and each region typically has three or four area offices. The Agency employs in excess of 9,000 staff.

Working as an environmental health officer

Most people who enter the environment industry as graduates work as environmental health officers (EHOs), or as environmental health technicians. You would enter a local authority as a technician and complete your environmental health officer training in that capacity (unless you opt to do a specific, accredited Environmental Health degree course followed by practical training as a student EHO).

Jobs and careers are available in local authorities, in agencies and with private companies, advising the company of their legal duties, helping them to maintain standards and liaising with local councils. Once you are qualified and have the appropriate experience, there are a growing number of consultancies being set up, where you would be self-employed and your work would include advising both private and public sector organisations.

Salaries vary, depending on whom you work for, but typically, a qualified EHO would get between £17,000 and £23,000 (at the time of writing), with a car allowance for using a private car for work. This is not a fixed figure, as EHOs working in different types of organisations are paid different salaries.

Environmental health became an issue – or rather the issue was addressed – in the last century. Poor water supplies, inadequate drainage and contaminated food caused disease and death, particularly in the overcrowded cities, during the industrial revolution. Since 1848, sanitary inspectors and public health inspectors – now collectively known as EHOs – have been inspecting, regulating and generally enforcing legislation in the areas of food control, health and safety at work, and housing.

Today's EHOs operate in these areas and also in the newer area of pollution and environmental protection. These are specialised professional jobs which require one science degree, at least, and sometimes two, in addition to the environmental health officer training and qualification from the Chartered Institute of Environmental Health. Environmental health technicians may also need a science degree.

Briefly, the areas you may work in will cover:

Housing:
- monitoring housing standards and taking action to ensure that houses are fit for habitation
- ensuring that the people living in the houses are safe from fire and other public health hazards, such as rats and infestation
- enforcement and prosecution (if necessary).

Health and safety at work:
- ensuring that working conditions are safe and healthy in working and recreational premises
- advising both employers and owners on how to maintain standards and how to protect workers and members of the public
- investigation of accidents
- enforcement and prosecution (if necessary).

Food control:
- ensuring that food is safe and edible, from production through to the end product (from abattoirs, through storage and distribution to shops and restaurants)
- advising businesses on food law and helping them to improve

- serving improvement notices
- shutting premises down in extreme cases
- running courses to educate food handlers
- raising consumer awareness of measures to prevent contamination in domestic situations.

Pollution and environmental protection:

- raising environmental awareness
- conducting environmental audits in local authorities
- checking levels of air, water, soil and noise pollution
- communicating the information to the appropriate people
- finding practical solutions to the problems of pollution
- land reclamation and identifying contaminated land.

A day in the life...

I moved into my job as an environment protection officer from being a hydrologist. My first degree was in hydrology, and my MSc was in waste water. I spend a fair amount of time out on site, in-specting sewage works and septic tanks, doing risk assessments and audits and explaining legislation and its implications to farmers and organisations. I work under my own steam, generally, but the job also involves meetings and negotiations with other professionals and with members of my team.

Being young, female and a representative of authority I have to work quite hard to be accepted by local farmers. They tend to take the line that they have been doing it their own way for years and can see no need to change – and what does a slip of a girl know about it anyway? Some cases are more difficult than others, but I usually manage to get the message across successfully. At times, too, I get tired of being seen as the enemy.

Being the kind of person who likes being active and outdoors, I find the paperwork – letters and writing-up – hard going. It's time-consuming and I think I make more of a meal of it than I need to. I'm going on a letter-writing course soon, which I hope will help. I was also sent on a communications course when I first started, which was extremely useful. Both courses have been paid for by the training department here. Otherwise, I haven't had specific training since I started the job. I enjoy my work – I'm interested in waste water and I'm fascinated by anything to do with science. I also enjoy talking to people and practical problem-solving.

Environmental protection officer, environmental agency

WORKING IN A LOCAL AUTHORITY

The majority of environmental health officers and landscape architects are employed by local authorities.

Environmental health officers will work either in generalised departments, responsible for all aspects of environmental health in a particular part of the area, or in specialist departments, working with a team responsible for specialist issues in that council's area, such as for example, air pollution, waste or food safety.

As this work is about maintaining standards and regulation, consistency of procedure and approach is essential, as is a thorough and up-to-date knowledge of legislation.

Working in local government has its advantages and disadvantages.

Historically, jobs in local government are secure and relatively well-paid, within a well-defined pay structure, with good pension schemes and holidays. This is still true, although restructuring and change has affected local government offices, and jobs are less secure than they were. The offices are run on more traditional lines than, for example, some of the newer charities and trusts might be, and the style and culture is generally more 'old fashioned' in outlook.

Council employees must, like Caesar's wife, be beyond reproach – and must be seen to be so. Correct procedures must be followed, and the hierarchy is carefully structured.

Of course, this is a generalisation and must be understood as such.

One interviewee pointed out that the running of the department depended on who was at the helm, and the approach of individual line managers.

It also depends on the kind of person you are, and whether the work you do is office-based. One person's constraints are another's security. Many of the people we interviewed had spent some time working in local government, had enjoyed it, and had gained valuable experience.

'When I left school with two arts A levels and secretarial skills, I wasn't sure what I wanted to do.

As I couldn't find a job right away, I stayed at home and did some voluntary work with children on environmental issues, which I enjoyed. That gave me a taste for working in the environment.

I then got a job in the administration department of a local council office, where I worked for environmental health officers and technicians. I saw the kind of work they did, and decided that was want I wanted to do.

I managed to complete an A level course in biology within a year, and I then went to university to do a BSc in Environmental Health, and was lucky enough to be sponsored by the borough council – there aren't many sponsorships, and there was a lot of competition.

I now work for them as an environmental health technician, dealing with all kinds of issues. I'm doing my practical training to become an EHO, completing a practical training logbook, and hope to sit my Chartered Institute of Environmental Health examinations at the end of this year to get my Certificate of Registration. Then I'll be a qualified EHO!

I really enjoy my work, the variety and the contact with people, although I found it challenging at first. I feel that I am doing some good.'

Environmental health technician, local government

WORKING IN THE VOLUNTARY SECTOR

Trusts and charities committed to the improvement of the environment generally work in partnership with all sectors of the local community, business and local government. The individual trusts often, but not always, operate as independent businesses or cost centres, and each has its own way of working within the scope and guidelines of the central body.

A few employees are taken on as permanent staff, but by far the majority of them are on short-term, one- to two-year contracts, working on specific projects.

The pay structure is arbitrary, as it depends on how much money is available for the project, and this can be a source of contention.

The management style is relaxed and friendly, the dress code in the offices we visited was relaxed, too – men had to wear a shirt or a shirt and tie and women were asked to be casual but smart (not jeans and a teeshirt, but no need for a formal suit).

'I trained as a civil engineer, and worked in a local authority's planning office in Lancashire for two years. I wasn't very happy doing that, so I left and did three months of volunteer work with youth groups before I was taken on as a ranger with the trust I work with now.

It was good to be working outdoors, but the pay was poor (£8,500 per year in 1997) and after a while I wanted involvement with the planning of projects.

Generally, you have to move around to move up in an organisation like this – project and contract work means you have to take the jobs where and when they come up. I got a job as a project officer in Leeds, which meant organisation and hands-on involvement in the project. The pay starts at about £10,500 per year for that, reaching £13,500. I really enjoyed it.

When the position of a project manager/team leader came up here, I applied and got it. The pay for that kind of position starts at about £16,000. I enjoy it, except for the bid-writing (writing proposals and bids for funding from the Government, the European Union and the Lottery, among others. The whole project has to be detailed and costed very carefully). I set up the project and then hand it on to two project officers to run with a team of volunteers. I miss the practical involvement and carrying a project through from beginning to end – it's quite hard letting go and allowing other people to run it, but I do have plenty to do otherwise, and I'm still involved in a practical capacity.

I'm very happy. If I wasn't, I'd go back to being a civil engineer and be unhappy on a lot more money!'

Project manager/team leader, environmental trust

Landscape architects

Change and modification of any environment must be made in as economic, sensitive and knowledgeable a way as possible, with input from any number of environment professionals, local council planners, civil engineers and members of the community.

Landscape architects often work in a team at the development stage of any project – whether it is designing a road, park, playground or shopping precinct. In rural areas, they may work on designs for agricultural and tourist landscapes.

Landscape architects will take the project through from feasibility studies to contracts, tendering, design and site inspections.

A day in the life...

I came into this job on a temporary basis from working in a local authority – my predecessor had gone on maternity leave and I stood in for her. By the time she came back, there was more than enough work for two of us, so I stayed. Before I went to university, I had found out about landscape architecture and had visited an architectural practice for a day, to get an idea of what it was like. I decided then that it was the profession for me.

I spend most of my time designing and drawing plans for recreation areas and parks, usually on reclaimed land. This gives me the opportunity to be creative, which I like. It is challenging, too, as I have to take account of a range of things as I design – environmental issues, community concerns, water, soil, drainage, and design within these constraints. I also have to attend quite a few meetings with local authority officers, developers, botanists, hydrologists, etc. as I can't begin the plans without consulting other experts. I may or may not see the project through from beginning to end, depending on whether I am working as part of a team on a large project, or on my own on a smaller, private one. I have to keep all the other project members informed and to attend team and project meetings. The work is varied, sometimes complex and sometimes frustrating, but that makes it more interesting.

It's important to keep up with what's happening around you, and to know what other people in the trust are doing and what's going on politically. Our trust also has a business department, so I do work for people in the private sector where the priorities are different, which is new. I enjoy my work and I expect to be doing much the same thing in a few years' time.

Landscape architect, environmental trust

WORKING IN WASTE MANAGEMENT

~~~ MYTH BUSTER ~~~

Waste management and caring for the environment are at opposite ends of the spectrum

Not so. Gone are the days when waste management was just about collecting and dumping rubbish – and making money out of it. Nowadays, it is a sophisticated industry whose purpose is not only to dispose of waste in an environmentally friendly way, but also to find ways of recycling or generating energy from it.

'Where there are people, there is waste. If people don't want landfill sites near them, then they should stop creating the waste in the first place. Our job is about damage limitation – and it's people who do the damage.'

Environmental officer, private waste management company

Waste management is another part of the environment industry that is growing rapidly. The challenge is to find environmentally friendly and economical ways of recycling and dealing with waste, such as identifying appropriate sites and designing landfill areas which allow the natural decomposing processes to occur. Access roads have to be constructed and careful thought goes into landscaping, the effect on the local population and the protection of water sources. Many landfill sites are extremely sophisticated, and the gases produced by the decomposition of the waste can be extracted and used to fuel power generators, creating electricity which can be sold to the National Grid. There is a need for more conservation of energy resources, so methods of generating energy from waste is a priority for research. It is a highly specialised and complex area, at the sharp end of engineering and scientific research, and it is growing fast.

More than 80,000 people are currently employed in the waste management industry. Half of them are employed by local authorities. A wide variety of interesting career opportunities are available in this industry in local authorities, agencies and private companies, so it is an area well worth considering. You can find out more about it by contacting the Institute of Wastes Management, see page 73.

'I was working as a civil engineer in a town council planning office before I joined this organisation. I was here right from the start, which meant that I could develop my own role. I wanted to do something interesting, new and exciting, and I'm glad I made the change. The work is varied and keeps me on my toes. I deal with all sorts of different people on a one-to-one basis – scientists, environmentalists, local authority people and ordinary people. I also attend meetings and sit on committees, and represent the agency by giving talks, answering questions and allaying anxieties. I manage the PR side of the business as well, which is a new area, and produce a newsletter.

I think I'm probably paid less than my counterparts at a similar level in the planning office, and a great deal less than I would be as a senior member of a private practice, but it's worth it. The only thing I'd change about it is the paperwork – there's a lot to do, and I don't enjoy it much. Otherwise I'm very happy.'

Senior manager, waste management company

'I am trained as an accountant, with two professional accountancy qualifications and an MBA. When I took the job of finance manager, a year ago, I was looking for variety and an opportunity to contribute more than just accountancy skills to the job I did, and I found it. My job involves working in the area of the Landfill Tax Credit Scheme, promoting it, raising awareness and looking for business. The scheme is a new one, and I enjoy the challenge of working in virgin territory, and generally creating and developing my own role.

As time goes on, I'd like to move further away from accountancy, and to concentrate on other areas. At the moment, I'm not interested in other jobs as this one is still challenging and interesting, but when I do think about it, I will have to look elsewhere in the field. The opportunities for promotion are non-existent in such a small "flat" organisation. I'm relatively badly paid but, for the moment, I'm willing to accept that in exchange for the satisfaction I get from the work.'

Finance manager, non-profit-making agency

We have looked at only a small selection of careers in different sectors of the environment industry. Obviously there are many more, ranging from clerical and administrative roles to specialist jobs for geologists and other environmental scientists. What is available to you is dependent on your skills and expertise, the area in which you want to live and work and the needs of the particular sector of the industry that interests you.

VITAL STATISTICS

Some of the case studies in this section have given an indication of salary levels for different jobs. The scope of the industry is so wide and the salary levels so diverse that it is not possible to give precise figures. However, it is true that salaries in this industry are not generally good. If you work in a large private organisation, you are more likely to earn more, but you will be expected to work longer hours to reflect your salary. Check out advertisements in the national press and on the Internet to get an idea of the going rates for the type of work in which you are interested.

Working conditions vary, but a flexible approach is expected as a rule. This can be interpreted in many different ways, and it is often up to the individual to regulate their own work, to a large extent. If you work additional hours, you cannot expect to be paid for it – and overtime rates are unheard of. Most organisations operate a time off in lieu (known as TOIL) system, as employees may have to attend public meetings in the evening or work on projects at the weekend. However, if you decide to take paperwork home, you may not be able to claim for extra work.

Neither is it easy to generalise about benefits packages offered by organisations, partly because they depend on the organisation's resources and attitude towards rewarding their staff, and partly because in this industry, they are often notable by their absence. If you are employed on a contract basis, there may be no benefits at all, and you will have to make your own arrangements if you want a pension and cover for sickness.

Ask for a detailed breakdown of what is offered so that you can weigh up a job offer with as much information as possible. Don't forget to find out the basis on which salaries and benefits increase (if there are any, and if they do!). Actual interview, you may want to ask:

- when salaries are reviewed
- how they are reviewed (are they performance related? based on an appraisal report? dependent on the project budget or the whim of your manager?)
- does holiday entitlement increase on an annual basis? (some organisations add a day to your entitlement for every year you are employed)
- will you be entitled to additional benefits once you have been with the company for a period of time?
- will the organisation help with travelling costs? (particularly important if you have to travel to sit on committees and attend meetings)
- are you expected to work outside office hours? If so, are you paid for overtime, does the organisation operate a TOIL system (time off in lieu) or do they just expect you to work over anyway?

part two the person

the person

Introduction

In Part One of *The Insider Career Guide to the Environment*, you looked at some of the jobs available in this area, the types of opportunities that could be available and the way that a few organisations or jobs work. Part Two focuses on you. Are you looking for the right kind of job in the right industry? What are employers looking for? What are the skills and personal qualities that would help you to succeed? In short, what kinds of people should be looking at a career in the environment, and are you one of them?

In the series of questions on the following pages, you'll be asked to assess yourself and the contribution you can make to any organisation. We focus particularly on the skills base and the qualities you might need to help you get into the work, to be able to do the work and to build up your career. This is summed up at the end in a skills audit, which you can use as a checklist.

KNOW YOURSELF

Getting a job and succeeding in your chosen career is about more than deciding what you want to do and waiting for a job to come knocking at your door. Jobs, and more particularly careers, in this industry are in demand and not easy to get into. You need to be prepared. Your skills and admirable qualities will not be evident to a prospective employer unless you can talk about them, demonstrate them or provide evidence that you can do them. You need to be able to market yourself.

The following self-assessment questionnaire gets you thinking about yourself in relation to the work that you want.

It will help you to make a start on:

- identifying what you want to do
- identifying what you don't want to do
- identifying what you can do, and what you are good at
- identifying what you cannot do, and areas for improvement.

For example, if you are an individualist and somebody who does not respond well to formal working structures, will you be happy working in a local council office where staff are expected to conform? Alternatively, if you like working steadily and knowing what you will be doing on a day-to-day basis, would you enjoy working within a new and changing organisation on a short-term contract? If your people skills are good, but you find written work difficult, would you be prepared to work hard to improve this aspect of your communication skills? These are some of the questions you may need to ask yourself.

The questionnaire that follows will also help you to build up a picture of your skills and qualities that you can use when you are completing a job application form, or in an interview. It will get you thinking about who you are and what you can contribute not only to the work, but also to a team or an organisation.

If you feel that you need more guidance, there are plenty of avenues you can explore:

- **Talk to careers advisers**. If you are still in education, you may be able to get help from your university or college careers service. Alternatively, talk to the staff at your local job centre to find out the services that are available; they vary across the country.
- **Find a reputable private careers guidance organisation**. Some of these offer a comprehensive service that will carry out an audit of your skills, attitudes, and experience to highlight areas that may suit you. They can also help you locate vacancies, prepare your CV, coach you for interviews and decide whether to accept a job. Choose a reputable organisation, find

out the range of services they offer and check their costs before you sign up for this sort of help. Some of them can be very expensive. You can find details of these organisations in careers literature, *Yellow Pages*, newspaper advertisements and on the Internet.

- **Check out literature** available in libraries and high street bookstores. There are plenty of books available that will help you self-audit, although this method is not guaranteed to give you impartial advice!
- **Talk to someone who works in the industry**. You may know someone who knows someone who works in the industry. Ask friends and relatives if they know anyone who can help. Insider information from the horse's mouth is always useful (if occasionally conflicting and confusing!) – as we found when researching this book.
- **Make contact with environmental organisations** and see if you can talk to someone already working there. People are usually very happy to be asked for advice and to give information – it gives them an opportunity to voice their opinions.

WHAT DO YOU WANT?

You need to look realistically at what you expect to get from your career and use that knowledge to determine what sort of jobs would be most appropriate for you. You could be looking for:

- work that interests you
- work with people
- outdoor work
- organisational and administrative work
- financial reward
- recognition for your talents
- friendship and a social life
- a challenge
- security
- variety
- the opportunity to develop new skills.

Answer the following questions. You don't need to write a book about yourself, simply make a note of the key points that come to mind as you consider each question. Not only will this exercise help clarify your thoughts, it will also help you to complete application forms and answer questions in an interview when you start looking for a job.

A.   Make your own list of at least six things that you would like from your job. When you have finished, go back and prioritise them, in the light of realistic expectations. You will probably have to compromise!

1. ....
2. ....
3. ....
4. ....
5. ....
6. ....

B.   Now identify three types of work that interest you. These could be specific jobs or broad areas such as 'work that brings me into contact with new people', or 'working outdoors'.

1. ....
2. ....
3. ....

C.   Now write down three things you definitely *don't* want to do! Again, these could be specific jobs or more general statements.

1. ....
2. ....
3. ....

Think about what you have read in Part One of this book. Did any of the work described attract you or put you off? Make a note of this.

Aspects that attracted you:

     1. ....

     2. ....

     3. ....

Aspects that did not attract you:

     1. ....

     2. ....

     3. ....

Did anything surprise you about what you found out? If it did, make a note of what it was, below and give yourself time to consider whether it has changed your thinking about going for a career in the environment industry.

....

....

....

....

What are your values?

The next thing to think about is your attitudes and values – do they fit in with the values you need for working with environmental issues. Answer yes or no to the following questions.

		Yes	No
1.	Are you concerned about environmental issues?	☐	☐
2	Do you know about trends in environmental thinking, new initiatives, Government directives?	☐	☐
3.	Do you like working outdoors?	☐	☐
4.	Do you like working with people?	☐	☐
5.	Are you ambitious?	☐	☐
6.	Do you want to earn a lot of money?	☐	☐

7. Are you really interested in your own area of work? ☐   ☐

8. Do you have an interest in Science and Geography? ☐   ☐

9. Are you looking for a formalised
    career structure? ☐   ☐

10. Do you have good communication skills? ☐   ☐

11. Are you looking for security? ☐   ☐

12. Do you want to climb the promotion ladder fast? ☐   ☐

13. Are you prepared to move to other organisations ☐   ☐
    and locations for better prospects?

How did you do?

If you answered yes to questions **1, 2, 3, 4, 7, 8, 10** and **13**, you have most of the attitudes and qualities essential for work in this area. If you answered yes to questions **6, 9, 11** and **12**, this may not be the industry for you. If you answered yes to question **5**, you need to think carefully about your choice. This is not to say that there is no place for ambitious, career-minded people, but opportunities to make it big are few and far between.

WHAT DO EMPLOYERS WANT?

Next we look at the skills and qualities you will probably need for work in the environment industry.

The following sentences have been taken from a variety of job advertisements in the environment and housing section of a national daily paper. We are all familiar with the words and phrases, but what do they actually mean?

In this section we look at some commonly used catch-all words and phrases that are likely to appear in advertisements and job descriptions, and consider what these terms mean in relation to yourself and to the environment industry.

'You will be **self-motivated**, highly professional, very committed to conservation and have **excellent inter-personal skills**.'

'A **highly motivated** and enthusiastic **team player** is sought to manage and develop our expanding and diverse community development activities.'

'You will need to be **self-motivated, willing** and **flexible** in your approach.'

'This is a challenging role, which will involve forming **effective working relationships** with a wide range of people. **Proactive and innovative**, you will be responsible for generating new ideas and delivering new environmental projects.'

'Excellent **communication and organisational skills** are essential.'

'The role requires **good inter-personal skills, strong communication skills** and experience of project management.'

'The role calls for **good teamworking and communication skills.**'

Communication skills

Communication is not just about talking. It involves getting a message across, making yourself understood and persuading, influencing or negotiating. To do this successfully, you need to:

- be able to express yourself concisely and clearly
- be assertive – say what you mean, say it with confidence, don't apologise for it but don't be aggressive
- think about your 'audience' – who they are, what they want or need to know, what their assumptions and understanding of the situation are
- LISTEN – communication is a two-way process, and you can't hope to communicate if you can't do this. A good old saying goes, 'Winners listen, losers wait for their turn to speak'. How many times have you met people who do this – and how frustrating is that?

Verbal communication skills

Whatever job you do, you must be able to communicate with other people. Dealing with the public, with other professionals, with officials, with volunteers and with team members is part of any work you do in this industry.

Many of the jobs involve raising awareness or educating the public, which means that you might be making presentations, explaining complicated legislation to resentful members of the public or talking in meetings. Advising, consulting, influencing, persuading and negotiating are also likely to be part of your work.

Written communication skills

The need to be able to write letters, write reports, write bids for funding and generally to keep people informed means that you really do need to be able to write competently. You don't have to be an academic or a novelist, but the ability to write clearly and appropriately is an advantage. Of course, you will learn as you go, and you can get to grips with any formats and conventions that apply by reading good examples of documents that have already been produced.

> 'When I was asked to write a letter to a client when I first started my "proper job", I agonised over it. I knew there were ways of writing business letters, but I couldn't remember what they were from school. I spent a whole day over the first words, thinking Dear Madam? – surely not! Dear Jenny? – too casual. Dear Mrs Jones? What if she's a Miss or a Ms? Is it faithfully or sincerely? Finally I asked someone to help – it was Ms and sincerely – but I hadn't realised how little I knew.'
> *Senior manager, waste management company*

Some employers offer training courses on written communication, as many people find it rigorous, especially if they have a science background where narrative skills are not generally needed.

Teamworking skills or being a good team player

Being a good team member combines a range of skills and personal qualities which help a team achieve a task or goal. Some of these are:

- being able to fit in without playing one-upmanship games, being competitive or stepping on other people's toes
- listening and respecting other people's views
- respecting the difference between your way of doing things and other people's ways

- showing consideration for other people
- knowing what is expected of you, and asking if you don't
- doing what you say you will do, when you say you will
- keeping people informed
- helping and supporting other people if they need it.

Teamworking may seem like the buzzword of the moment, but it has become an essential part of working life. Organisations rely on their staff working together to produce results. Individual initiative and leadership are still very important qualities, but you do have to be able to work with others and to put your team's needs above your own.

Almost all the organisations we researched work with team structures, seeing this as a way to maximise staff resources, share knowledge and learning, and reinforce co-operation. If you don't respond well to being part of a group and working with other people, then think again about whether you will be able to adapt to the culture of this type of organisation.

Graduates may find teamworking one of the hardest skills to develop. Studying for a degree at university, particularly in more traditional disciplines, emphasises individual academic achievement. Consequently, practical group culture and team skills can be alien concepts and making the transition to work in a culture where these factors dominate is very difficult.

Some organisations offer training to help employees to develop teamworking skills – but don't bank on it. However, it is necessary to ask yourself if you have the personal attributes that will make you a team player.

Inter personal skills or forming effective working relationships

Usually, this means a combination of teamworking skills and communication skills, as well as just getting on with people in general. Added to these are:

- being able to talk easily to strangers
- being able to maintain different kinds of relationships with the people you meet or work with

- knowing what your role is, behaving appropriately and knowing where your boundaries are
- dealing reasonably and calmly with conflict, disagreement and confrontation
- negotiating with people and being able to compromise
- asking for what you want or asking people to do things without being bossy, manipulative or apologetic.

Your interpersonal skills will be put to the test if you move into a management role, and this could happen quickly in a smaller agency or trust.

Leadership skills

Being able to lead a team is about communication (again), organisation, inter-personal skills, practical problem-solving and decision-making skills, all of which you may already have. Confidence in your ability, respect for other people, flexibility and a willingness to learn are the bases upon which leadership skills are built.

Unless management skills or experience are specifically required for the position you are applying for, you won't be expected to know all about them. There are whole libraries of books available on the various management skills. Check out your library or bookshop, in the business books or management skills section.

Organisational skills

This can mean several things, and usually means all of them: organising and planning work, and organising people to do the work. You need to be able to:

- know what you are doing, and when
- plan the work in advance
- break the work down into different tasks
- assign tasks to people appropriately and fairly
- check that it is all going smoothly
- re-organise if necessary
- follow up.

Organisation of facts, accuracy and attention to detail are particularly important for environmental health officers in all sectors. Your investigations may have a substantial impact on people's lives and livelihoods, and could lead to a court case, so it is essential to be accurate and precise.

Self-motivated

Sometimes the term 'self-starting' is used in advertisements. Both mean being able to use your initiative and work on your own without being told what to do. It may also mean that the organisation is under-staffed and poorly managed – which can either work for or against you, depending on how you work.

Most jobs in this industry require you to work on your own for some of the time. Even if you work as part of a team, you are likely to be responsible for your own area of work and to be expected to get on with it. This will be extremely difficult to do when you first begin a job, and you will have to ask a lot of questions. But as your confidence increases, so will your ability to use your discretion, make sound judgements and go it alone.

As you work your way up the career ladder, decision making becomes increasingly important and some of the decisions you make could have a major impact on others. Responsible decision making, based on an analysis of all the information available and the current situation, is a key skill.

Proactive

Proactive behaviour is the opposite of reactive behaviour – reacting to circumstances or events. A proactive person initiates action rather than waiting for events to happen, then reacting to them. This goes hand in hand with using your initiative or being self-motivated. In any industry, it is one of the qualities that separates achievers from the rest.

Flexible/adaptable

A flexible approach to your work is one where you have to change your plans to fit in with other people. The statement 'flexible working hours' in an advertisement can mean that you can chose to work your hours as you please, within reason. Formalised flexible working, where you work so many hours per week with flexibility built in, will be called flexitime. Usually, 'flexible working' means that you are expected to work over and above the stated hours, if necessary (and if it is in print, you will definitely be expected to do so).

The ability to adapt to changing conditions, and to be flexible is essential in a growing and changing industry. New initiatives, legislation and funding opportunities, both nationally and from the European Union, all have a significant impact on the industry, whether it is in the public or in the private sector. On top of that, many of the organisations you are likely to work in may be fairly new and small, and the personnel and management frameworks and structures (if any!) may still be having teething problems. Obviously this does not apply to Government bodies and departments, but local government procedures and practices are changing in some areas, and change is in the air.

Geographical flexibility is also essential if you want to make your way up a career ladder. Permanent positions are available in all sectors, but many of the jobs in trusts or charities are dependent on funding for particular projects, which means having to move around the country.

'You have to follow the jobs and projects around if you want to progress. I've moved across the country three times in the last four years. Two of the positions I've held have been with the same trust, but you can't count on moving up within a particular organisation. I hope that when the project I'm working on now comes to an end, I'll be able to start on another within this trust, or get a permanent position here.'

Trust project manager

Highly motivated

Highly motivated people are committed to their work. This phrase can also be translated as the less acceptable word 'ambitious', but ambitious sounds pushy. It may also mean that you will have to be highly motivated to put up with the stress and strain of the job.

Commitment comes high on the list of desirable qualities for environment industry recruits. As has been mentioned before, almost everyone we interviewed was committed to caring for the environment. Employers will be looking for this as a necessary requirement.

Keeping up with environmental issues is another facet of commitment and motivation, viewed by recruiters as basic to any environment industry job. From before your interview, if you have one, to the end of your career in this area, things will be changing in the industry. Your job, whatever it is, will follow the ramifications and growing pains of a growth industry. Changes in legislation are bound to have an impact on your work and, in your likely role as advisor and educator, you will also need to keep your knowledge-base up to date.

'In our place, the telephone conversations everywhere are all, Have you heard about. . ? What do you think about. . ? Can you tell me what's happening with. . ? Who's the contact for. . ?'

Director, regeneration association

Innovative

This usually means that you are expected to have new, bright and creative ideas and to do things in new ways. An innovative approach to problem solving may apply to both the environmental issues you work with and to managing your work or team. Many organisations in this sector are small and work to tight budgets. Running the show, managing resources and producing results at any level can demand a great deal of creativity and lateral thinking!

So far, we have looked at a range of skills and qualities that are basic requirements for anyone considering a career in the environment industry. Technical skills and specialist knowledge will vary with the job you do, but depending on the type of job you apply for, you may also need to have or to be able to demonstrate the following. . .

Willingness to work outdoors

Many jobs require you to work outdoors and to participate in physical activities. This does not necessarily mean being out enjoying the fresh air – you could be inspecting a blocked drain, investigating vermin infestations or walking around chemical factories as an EHO, or helping with work on a land reclamation site in other roles. If you want to work in a warm and cosy office all day, you might find that work in the environment is not your cup of tea.

Computer literacy and keyboard skills

These are also required skills in many organisations in the industry, although they may not be formally stated. Most people in work at present are able to use a computer and operate the 'hunt and peck' typing system at varying levels of competence. If you have any time at all, it is worth enrolling on a basic word-processing or keyboard course if you can't use a computer. These are often available as evening classes from local colleges of further education, with special rates and concessions for various groups of people. It will save time and frustration in the long run.

'If there's one thing I could have had some training in, I would have chosen keyboard skills. I still have to write out my longer reports in longhand, give them to a secretary to type out, correct them, give them back, check and sign them – then finally I can send them off. It feels like such a waste of time, but it takes me too long to do it myself on the computer.'

Environmental health officer

Financial awareness

This is not so important for some work as it is for others. The emphasis in the various central and local government offices and bodies is not particularly on financial considerations, although this is becoming much more of an issue.

If you are working in a trust or charity or in the private sector, you will need to have some idea about budgets and funding. You won't be expected to understand the ins and outs of how the finances work if you join at a relatively lowly level, but you'll be working within a limited budget, and will be expected to remember that. You are likely to have to work in as economical and cost-effective way as possible.

Driving

You will probably need to be able to drive, and you may be asked to use your own car for work-related travel, if public transport is not available.

> 'I try to use public transport as much as possible, but sometimes, unfortunately, it just isn't an option. If I didn't have a car, I wouldn't be able to do my job.'
>
> Trust education officer

SKILLS AUDIT

This checklist sums up the information on the personal qualities and skills needed for work in the environment already given in this section.

As a self-check, you may want to ask yourself: Is this me? as you read through the following points. Go through them and tick the statements that you think apply to you. Remember that not *all* of them are likely to be relevant to you!

Even more useful is to get someone else who knows you well to read through them, too, deciding whether you have the qualities and skills listed. You can then discuss your conclusions. Between you, you will develop a pretty good idea of the things you are good at – and the things you are not so good at. You may also find out something about yourself. Everyone carries around assumptions about their qualities and skills which are not always reflected in the way that other people see them.

Communication skills

Do you:

	Yes	No
Express yourself concisely and clearly?	☐	☐
Say what you mean, confidently, without being apologetic or aggressive?	☐	☐

Communication skills *continued*
Do you:

	Yes	No
Think about the people you are addressing, their agenda and level of understanding?	☐	☐
Listen?	☐	☐
Generally manage to persuade people to your way of thinking?	☐	☐
Exert influence over people?	☐	☐

Teamworking skills
Do you:

	Yes	No
Fit in to groups and teams?	☐	☐
Listen and respect other people's views?	☐	☐
Respect the difference between your way of doing things and other people's ways?	☐	☐
Show consideration for other people?	☐	☐
Know what is expected of you?	☐	☐
Ask if you don't know what is expected of you?	☐	☐
Do what you say you will do, when you say you will?	☐	☐
Keep people informed?	☐	☐
Help and support other people if they need it?	☐	☐

Inter personal skills
Do you:

	Yes	No
Talk easily to strangers?	☐	☐
Maintain different kinds of relationships with the people you meet?	☐	☐
Behave appropriately and know where your boundaries are?	☐	☐
Deal reasonably and calmly with conflict, disagreement and confrontation?	☐	☐

Inter personal skills *continued*

Do you:

	Yes	No
Negotiate and compromise?	☐	☐
Ask people to do things without being bossy, manipulative or apologetic?	☐	☐

Organisational skills

Think about a situation when you have had to carry out a job or task, or a piece of work.

Did you:

	Yes	No
Know what you were doing, and when?	☐	☐
Plan work or events in advance?	☐	☐
Break work down into different tasks?	☐	☐
Assign tasks to people appropriately and fairly, if necessary?	☐	☐
Regularly check that things were going smoothly?	☐	☐
Re-organise if necessary?	☐	☐
Follow up?	☐	☐

Other qualities and skills

	Yes	No
Do you use your initiative and get on with things?	☐	☐
Can you work on your own without being told what to do?	☐	☐
Are you prepared to change your plans to fit in with other people?	☐	☐
Do you often do more than is necessary or expected of you in certain situations?	☐	☐
Do you initiate action rather than waiting for something to happen?	☐	☐
Do you have bright and creative ideas and do things in new ways?	☐	☐
Are you committed to caring for the environment?	☐	☐
Are you interested in current environmental issues?	☐	☐

Other qualities and skills *continued*

	Yes	No
Do you easily adapt to change?	☐	☐
Would you be prepared to move around the country for work?	☐	☐
Are you usually accurate and precise, paying attention to detail?	☐	☐
Are you able to make speedy, well-informed decisions?	☐	☐
Do you want to work outdoors and to participate in physical activities?	☐	☐
Can you communicate clearly and appropriately in writing?	☐	☐
Can you use a computer?	☐	☐
Do you feel confident that you could lead a team in a work situation?	☐	☐
Are you good with finances (including your own?)	☐	☐
Can you drive?	☐	☐

The ticks in the *No* boxes indicate the gaps in your knowledge or skill-base. You may be able to develop these areas, either on your own, on a course or evening class or from one of the many excellent short books you will find in the business and management section of any large bookshop.

Now that you have read through this part of the book, you should have built up a profile of your own skills and qualities, matched with the skills and qualities that employers are looking for.

In the next section, *Getting in, Getting on… Getting out*, you will be looking at making applications and going to interviews. You may want to draw on the self-knowledge you have gained when you are considering these.

part three

getting in, getting on… getting out

getting in, getting on... getting out

Introduction

The third part of *The Insider Career Guide to the Environment* focuses on how you can get into the industry, how you can get on and climb the career ladder and how, if necessary, you can get out and take a new direction.

The job market in general is highly competitive and this industry is no exception. There are a lot of enthusiastic and highly qualified people out there seeking a limited number of positions. Competition is particularly fierce when it comes to getting into the environment industry in the first place.

How can you make your application stand out from the rest so that you get past the initial stages of selection and into an interview? A little inside knowledge can go a long way towards helping you prepare an application that will be noticed. If you are invited to an interview, you can improve your performance by understanding what the selectors are looking for and following some simple advice to upgrade your interview technique.

Once you have found the opportunity you want, how might your career take shape – and do you actually want a career? What prospects are there for advancement within the various environmental sectors? We look at opportunities for promotion and advancement.

Finally if, after a period of working in the environment industry, you decide that you want to move on to something new, the experience and skills you have gained could prove invaluable in other industries. What would you do next?

Read on to find out.

We look, first, at some of the routes into the industry from a variety of starting points, and at the qualifications, qualities and experience you may need.

QUALIFICATIONS

A degree in Earth Sciences, Geography, Geology, Botany or one of the other more specialised sciences is desirable if you want to take up a professional career. There is a lot of competition, and often a first degree is not enough to get you in other than at a fairly junior level. Experience also counts – many of the professionals who work in the industry have moved over from other areas, such as local government, engineering or straight accountancy.

On the other hand, a degree or even a postgraduate degree does not automatically make you a desirable recruit for entry into some of the less formal organisations. With just a few GCSEs, including Maths, Science and English, you can join a charity or trust and work your way up, as long as you have done your time as a volunteer.

Starting from scratch – volunteer work

Whether you have a degree or just a few GCSEs, you can start your career in the environment as a volunteer. Many of the trusts and charities expect applicants to have volunteer experience. Although it is not always stated as a requirement, all the people working in the trusts and charities that we interviewed had done a stint of volunteer work, and all of them said that it was essential. It is generally understood to be a requirement and it is one of the most popular ways into this area of work, whether you are highly qualified or not. Having a degree or even two degrees does not mean that you can walk into a job, as practical experience or post-graduate training is often a necessary additional requirement. Applicants who have spent time doing volunteer work will be considered above those who have not, even if their paper qualifications are not so good. It not only gives you an insight into the kind of work available, what goes on and how things are done, but also – and probably more importantly – demonstrates your commitment and enthusiasm.

Most charities and trusts depend on volunteer workers. Volunteers can be involved in many different areas, including:

- education (work with schoolchildren, youth work and awareness raising in the community). An example of this would be running projects with schoolchildren who will carry out an assessment of their own school on its waste and energy management processes, resulting in their making recommendations for improvement, savings and recycling
- community projects (working with communities and local business to inform them and to involve local people in environmental projects). This is part of the Government's drive for social inclusion, regeneration and the New Deal for Communities. In the words of one team leader:

'People want to be involved in the improvement of their own environment. They don't want marvellous schemes thought up by strangers thrust upon them, and it doesn't work. And we don't just want to involve the community – we want to be part of it, and the community to be part of us'.

- landscape architecture
- administration.

...in fact, in every aspect of the work of the trust.

'I worked in a casino for eight years before I decided that I wanted a career in the environment. Not only did I have to work to put myself through a degree in agro-forestry, but I also had to finance my volunteer work. I couldn't have got into this job without having done that. I advise anyone who might want to do this kind of work to be a volunteer during school holidays or university vacations, if they can.'

Education officer, large voluntary organisation

Find out about volunteer work in your area by contacting the larger organisations at their headquarters or websites (some addresses are given at the end of this book), looking in the *Yellow Pages* of your local phone book or asking at the local library, which may have details of the schemes available.

Starting from the bottom

There are a few technician level, clerical and administrative and practical jobs that you can enter with four or five GCSEs (including subjects relevant to the post). For example, you would need to have English and Maths at grade C or above for an administrative post, along with a science and relevant skills such as word processing or book-keeping. Jobs may be available:

- in the Civil Service – in the local Department of the Environment Office
- in local government – the council environmental health offices
- in the voluntary sector (but you are likely to have to enter as a volunteer).

You may be able to find out about training with an employer in the environment industry from your local job centre.

Working as a warden

∧ MYTH BUSTER ∧

You can start your career as a warden or ranger – you don't need qualifications to do that

There are two popular misconceptions in this statement. One is the assumption that a warden's position is necessarily at the bottom of a career ladder. It isn't. Most wardens want to carry on being one, and are usually more interested in a footpath than a career path. You can progress by becoming a ranger, but those wardens with a permanent position are not going to give it up that easily in the teeth of the very fierce competition. Which brings us to the second point – we have already said that competition is generally fierce in the environment industry, but these jobs are like gold-dust!

Volunteer wardens are a different matter – there are many more of these positions on offer, and that *can* lead to a career.

The job titles of warden and ranger are often used to mean the same thing. Here, we distinguish the two:

- wardens – are concerned with the day-to-day practical aspects of looking after a park, forest, estate, etc.
- rangers – liaise with the relevant authority, deal with the public and take on a more administrative role.

Formal academic qualifications are not always required for these popular, practical outdoor jobs. Experience as a volunteer of estate work or of forestry is essential, as is a commitment to conservation and general physical fitness. There is often a minimum age limit of 21.

The National Trust offers Careerships in gardening and countryside warden work, a three-year training course leading to an NVQ at level 3. The Trust will be happy to give you more details if you are interested. A word of warning – fewer than 20 positions are available each year. Don't be put off by this, you could be one of them; but you will have to convince the Trust of your suitability for the course, your commitment and your willingness to work hard. Forget it if you think you might quite like it, but are not sure.

Working as a countryside ranger

If you manage to find a job as a ranger, you may then be able to move into a more senior position. This extract from a job advertisement for a senior ranger in an urban park gives you a flavour of the kind of position you could be looking for if you want to progress:

> **Senior countryside ranger**
> £17,500 – £20,400
> The partnership is seeking a senior countryside ranger with a variety of general and specialist skills in urban conservation and countryside management. The senior ranger will be responsible for reviewing and co-ordinating all aspects of the site's management and business plans, as well as facilitating staff rotas, patrolling sites and promoting the county park.

... which won't leave you much time to be alone with your thoughts and the land!

Entering the industry with A levels or a degree

Most of the jobs available in the industry are taken by graduates, so if you have A levels – particularly in sciences or Geography – you would be well advised to go to college or university and get a degree.

If you do manage to get a job, you may want to consider completing an NVQ level 3 or 4 in Environmental Conservation. These are accredited by COSQUEC (see page 71).

Training as an environmental health officer at 18+

Training to be an environmental health officer is a rigorous and relatively long process. There are several ways of doing this, but the following gives you an outline of how you might complete your training starting from when you leave school.

You will need to have science A levels or equivalent BTEC qualifications to get on to an accredited BSc in Environmental Health/Science degree course. There are only a few of these courses available, and it is important that the course you enrol on is accredited by the CIEH (Chartered Institute of Environmental Health). If it isn't, you cannot qualify as an EHO. Contact the CIEH for its information pack, which will give you up-to-date details of these courses (see page 72). Entry requirements differ, and most universities and colleges are flexible about the requirements if you are a mature student, so you will have to check with the individual universities.

You will have to undergo both academic and practical training to achieve the qualification, and you can do that either by completing a full three-year degree course followed by 48 weeks of practical training, often while you are employed as a technical officer, or by doing a sandwich course which integrates the two.

The following is an example of the kind of job advertisement you will be looking for so that you can complete your practical work:

Degree sponsorship opportunity
Technical officer/Student environmental health officer
Salary £6,739 to £7,861

We have a vacancy in the pollution control section of the department for a person who wishes to qualify as an environmental health officer and already has an appropriate scientific/environmentally based background. As part of this post you will attend, on a part-time basis, the BSc(Hons) Environmental Health course at the City College, or consideration will be given to students in possession of a degree in Environmental Health who have yet to complete their practical training.
   The academic requirements are 18 points at A level (including one science) or an equivalent BTEC qualification.

Once you have completed this, and qualified, you can sit the CIEH (Chartered Institute of Environmental Health) professional exams to qualify as an EHO. You cannot become an EHO without passing these exams, which comprise:

- five written case study papers
- a risk audit
- an interview.

When you have been through this process, you will be a fully-qualified environmental health officer.

Training as a landscape architect

You can complete your training as a landscape architect in two ways. You can either complete a post-graduate degree or diploma course which must be accredited by The Landscape Institute (see page 74). If you do this, your first degree must be in a related subject, such as Architecture, Horticulture or Botany. It is advisable that you also have relevant work experience before beginning your second degree, but you may be able to go straight into it.

   The second option is to complete a degree course in Landscape Architecture from school. The entry requirements for this are two A levels or their equivalent in related subjects, such as Art, Botany, Geography and natural science subjects. You will also need GCSEs in English and Science and Maths. If you are studying full-time, you will be expected to complete a three year Honours course before doing one year of practical work. After that you will complete your Part IV or MSc one year course to become a fully-fledged landscape architect.

What kind of degree?

If you do not want to follow the routes we have outlined above, and become an EHO or a landscape architect, you need to give careful consideration to the kind of degree courses you will take.

'The one word of advice I'd give someone thinking of a degree to help them get into a career in the environment is *specialise*. If you can do a specific science degree, do it. If you do a general science degree, such as Biology, find a specific subject for your dissertation.'

Environment protection officer with a BSc in Hydrology and an MSc in Waste Water

This advice is good, but be aware that it may limit your choice and employability elsewhere when you come to look for a job.

Degrees in Geography, Geology and Biological Sciences offer a solid basis for an environmentally oriented career, if you do not want to specialise. It is possible to enter with another kind of degree, but a Geology graduate has much more chance of succeeding than a Philosophy graduate. That said, there are other areas of work, and our interviewees came from a wide variety of backgrounds. Other than those who had degrees and second degrees in Hydrology and Agro-forestry, or with specialised degrees in Landscape Architecture, people came in from the following backgrounds, amongst others:

- civil engineering, with experience in local government (there were several of these)
- structural engineering, with industry experience
- accountancy, with work experience (there were several of these)
- technical drawing, with experience as a technician

- PR, with work experience
- administration and management experience
- teaching, with work experience.

You will see from this short list that the common denominator is experience. If your experience is relevant to the post advertised, you will be considered, whatever your background. However, that does not help you very much if you are just out of university.

WORK EXPERIENCE

If you are just about to start your career, a period of work experience (as opposed to volunteer experience) can be an invaluable way of finding out if you have chosen the right field of employment. Work experience has become an integral part of secondary school education; it not only allows students to find out more about different jobs, it also educates them in the harsh realities of working life. The need for some ready cash has encouraged many young people to take part-time and vacation work or to spend their gap year in full-time employment. Consequently, most students have some experience of work before they take the plunge and apply for their first permanent job.

The amount of training and/or experience that people need before they can effectively contribute to environmental work means that it is not economical for organisations to take on weekend and temporary staff.

Work experience with any environment-oriented organisation, where you have had contact with the public or where you have worked as part of a team, will stand you in good stead. If you have done any of this kind of work, don't forget to refer to it on application forms or when you are being interviewed.

WORK PLACEMENTS

If you are still at school or university and are considering a career in the industry, you might want to apply for a period of work experience or a work placement with one of the trusts or charities. Not all charities operate these programmes, but those that do will offer a two- to three-month placement during the summer months.

The content and format of these programmes differ widely. Some are structured so as to get you involved in projects and include elements of training. With other placements, you may just be shadowing and accompanying an experienced member of staff to find out what they do, as well as making tea, photocopying, making phone calls, etc.

Competition for placements is stiff but if you can get a place it will benefit you enormously by:

- improving your knowledge of the industry
- helping you understand the culture of these organisations and the type of people who work there; this will help you decide if it is right for you
- giving you an edge over other applicants who are applying for jobs. What more appropriate work experience could you quote on your CV than a period already spent working in the industry?

If you want a work placement, be prepared to fight for it. Many other students would like one, too. Start searching for appropriate placements as early as possible. Make initial approaches at the beginning of the autumn term for a placement during the following summer. To help you with your search, you could:

- check with your university careers service to find out if they have details of placements
- identify at least six organisations you could approach
- read through appropriate job vacancy pages in national newspapers and in specialist magazines and publications to find out about these organisations and the services they offer
- contact organisations you are interested in and ask if they operate work placement schemes
- when you identify the scheme you want to apply for, get a named contact with whom you can liaise.

A key recommendation of the Dearing Committee was that companies expand their work experience and sponsorship schemes. According to the Association of Graduate Recruiters, at the beginning of 1998, 40% of its members were offering sponsorship places. Check out some of the private sector organisations that interest you on the Internet; if they do have these opportunities, you will find further details of how to apply.

Other skills and experience that are relevant to this type of work and could, therefore, make your application more effective are:

- evidence of computer literacy; you should be able to use a PC
- some experience in working with customers. This could be in any field of employment. What recruiters are interested in is your ability to interact confidently with the public (face to face and on the telephone), to be helpful and polite at all times
- teamworking skills
- organisational skills.

As we have already said, one of the key features of a successful job application is the ability to provide evidence that supports your claims. Anybody can walk into an interview and say that they are good with people, love working with their colleagues and are highly organised in their approach to routine tasks. What the selector wants to see is evidence of these skills.

During your time at school or college, when you work in part-time, voluntary or vacation jobs, you will begin to develop a skills and experience base. Use the following checklist to help you identify things you have done which show you possess the skills you will need. If you have not had any actual work experience in these areas, think of other general interest or leisure activities or parts of your course-work that might have generated evidence and that you can expand on.

People skills	Work experience or part-time and vacation work in any retail outlet Voluntary work
Teamworking skills	Activities at school/college Committee work, sports, voluntary or community work
Written communication skills	Your degree course dissertation Any administrative or letter-writing work you may have done for voluntary or leisure activities
Organisational skills	Organising committees School/college-based project work Organising rotas for staff in your part-time job.

GETTING IN

Unless you have very influential contacts, or your reputation is so good that you are headhunted, you will have to make a formal application for a job. In the early stages, this involves either completing an application form or submitting your CV and a letter of application answering the advertisement to the organisation you want to work for. If you pass the preselection stages and the selectors think you have the skills, qualifications and experience they need, you will be called for an interview.

Your application form, if there is one, CV and covering letter are the first point of contact with prospective employers so it is important that you get them right. First impressions are very important, and the way that you present yourself and your application is vital. One job advertisement can stimulate hundreds of responses, most of which will be rejected almost immediately.

'The response was terrific. When the application letters and CVs started to pour in, I realised that I'd have to be brutal. Some people had just sent in a CV without a covering letter. They went first. Then I rejected the ones with scrappy, handwritten CVs and letters with obvious spelling mistakes. Then we started!'

Recruiter for an agency

Employers don't have the time or resources to interview everybody who wants to work for them, so they will be ruthless in weeding out any applications that do not meet their selection criteria.

The job market, particularly for this industry, is very competitive. The organisation wishing to fill one vacancy may receive hundreds of applications for the position. Your application needs to be focused towards the industry and you will improve your chances of being considered for it if you can show in your letter that you know something about the area in which you want to work. Spend time finding out about the organisation – you can phone and ask them to send you any relevant literature they may have.

The Insider guide to completing application forms

- Give yourself plenty of time; you cannot expect to complete an application form well if you try to fill it in during a spare half hour.
- Read through *all* the questions first.
- Write your rough copy up on a separate piece of paper or, if you can, photocopy the form and use the copy as a rough draft. Get the details down on your rough copy before you even think about starting on the original.
- Make sure you do exactly what you are asked to do. If the form asks you to list your education in chronological order, start with your secondary school and work through to your most recent college or university course. If it asks for details of past employment in reverse chronological order, start with your most recent job.
- Answer the questions honestly; don't make claims you cannot substantiate. Interviewers may use what you have written as a basis for asking questions, and expect you to be able to expand on it.
- Get your facts straight. Check dates, particularly of periods of education and employment, and try not to leave unexplained gaps.

- Always try to give evidence of your skills and achievements. Employers want to know what you have done and can do now, not what you *think* you can do.
- Check your spelling, grammar and punctuation. Better still, get somebody else to check them for you.
- Use black ink to complete the original form. It may be photocopied by the selectors and lilac, silver and green ink do not come through clearly; neither do they look professional.
- Make sure you submit the form before the closing date.
- Keep a record of your submission date and where you sent it to.
- Keep a copy of the form or letter; it can be useful if you need to make an application elsewhere.
- If you don't hear anything after a couple of weeks, phone to find out what has happened to your application.

The Insider guide to writing effective CVs

- Keep a record of any information that could be relevant to a job application. Use this as the basis of your CV.
- Don't think that you can send the same CV out for every job for which you apply. Different employers and different jobs demand a different blend of the same skills and qualities. Tailor your CV to meet the needs of any job specification you receive. Pick out the key words and try to match them with experience you can offer.
- Follow the same advice as for application forms – give evidence to support any claims you make about your skills and experience.
- Keep your CV reasonably short: two pages of A4 paper should be long enough. If it is much longer, you may be including irrelevant information.
- Draft print a copy and check the spelling, punctuation and grammar. Don't rely on your computer software to check it for you.

- Use good quality, white A4 paper for the final copy.
- Print your CV or get somebody to print it for you. It should be letter quality from an inkjet or laser printer.

Explore different ways of writing your CV. A style and format suitable for one person or job may not be appropriate for another. If you are just leaving school, college or university, then a straightforward chronological account of your education and work experience, together with some information on your interests and any responsible positions you have held will be fine.

If you have more to say, ask yourself what the person on the receiving end will be looking for and, if you can, organise the content to reflect their needs. In the past, CVs were always written in chronological order, but today they tend to be written for the reader. That means that a mature applicant with a list of several jobs and responsibilities would present the reader with what they need to know at the beginning – start with the job you hold at present and work backwards. Employers are not as interested in what you might have done five years ago as they are in what you are currently doing. If you are changing jobs, you could use a different format which highlights relevant past job roles or focuses on your skills and technical expertise. There are dozens of good books on the market that will help you to develop an effective CV. Buying one could be a useful investment, or borrow one from a library.

The Insider guide to writing effective covering letters

You must include a covering letter with your application form or CV. This should state:

- the job you are applying for
- where you heard about the vacancy, or the name and date of a newspaper advertisement (employers use this information to monitor the success of their recruitment campaigns)

- why you think you are a suitable candidate for the job. This should be no more than a short paragraph highlighting areas of experience or relevant skills that you have mentioned in your CV or application form.

Your letter should also include a closing paragraph in which you invite further contact from the employer. For example, 'I look forward to hearing from you soon.'

Again, follow the guide for producing a CV: use good quality white paper, and an inkjet or laser printer.

If, rather than responding to an advertised vacancy, you are sending out a speculative letter to an organisation to find out if they might be interested in you, get a named contact before you start your correspondence. Ring the head office of the organisation and ask to be put in contact with the personnel or human resources department. When you get through to them, ask for the name of the person to whom you should write. Try to get additional information about what they are looking for in new staff and how the company structures its selection process.

The Insider guide to performing well at interviews

Interviews are a two-way process. They help the employer to find out if you are the best person for the job and they help you to find out more about the position and to make up your mind if this is the job you want. Most people feel nervous before an interview; after all, there is a lot at stake. If you are willing to spend some time preparing for the event, that can go a long way towards improving the interview experience. It will also will increase your confidence so that you are able to present yourself more positively when you meet the selectors.

Here is a very brief guide to good interview techniques. If you are just starting your career, or have not experienced many interviews, invest in a book about interview skills. There are plenty of good titles available which offer useful and detailed advice to help you improve the communication skills you will need when you talk to a prospective employer.

Before the interview:

- Take time and prepare as thoroughly as you can.
- Read the recruitment literature carefully. What does it tell you about the people who work there, the way things are done and the feel of the place?
- Find out all you can about the organisation you are applying to. Look at brochures detailing its purpose or mission, its websites, if appropriate, and try to find out about its past achievements, structure, funding and anything else you can get your hands on.
- Research the vacancy. What does the work involve? How will your experience and skills help you meet the demands of the job? Again, look carefully at the job description or outline, if you have the information. Something can be gleaned from the way the advertisement is worded and presented.
- Find out how the interview will be conducted: will you be interviewed by one person or a panel? Do you have to take any tests? How long will the whole process take? If you don't know, ring up the contact on the advertisement and find out.
- Think about the questions you might be asked, and prepare your answers. Can you produce evidence to support any statements you make, or that you have made in your application about what you can do? We can all claim to be good leaders; the selector will want to know about a particular time when you demonstrated your leadership skills.
- If you can't answer, don't know or if you've gone blank, say so. That way you are likely to be seen as disarmingly honest rather than embarrassed and ignorant!
- Think about the questions *you* want to ask. Remember, the interview is a time for you to collect information too, and you will look like a more attractive applicant if you are interested enough to ask questions. You could ask about the organisation, how work is done, who you might be working with.
- Read up on current and relevant Government

initiatives (see the DETR website for an outline of what is going on at present) and read any (current!) issues of environmental magazines to find out what is going on. Your enthusiasm and commitment to environmental issues will be noted. For details of contact addresses, websites and magazines, see *Want to find out more?*

- Remember that the interviewer's purpose is to find out about you, not to catch you out.

During the interview:

- Wear appropriate clothes and check that you are well-groomed. Dressing for success may be a cliché, but your appearance is important and is something on which you will be judged. The Civil Service, local government offices and agencies will expect you to be smart and conservative, so wear a suit. Other organisations may be less formal, but even if you walk in to find that they are all sitting around in jeans and woolly jumpers, a suit will still be appropriate. People expect you to make an effort.

- Be punctual. Give yourself plenty of time to cope with rush-hour traffic and train delays. If you have an early interview and have to travel some distance, think about travelling the night before and staying over. If you are unavoidably delayed, try to phone to explain what has happened.

- Sit quietly for a few minutes before your interview. Empty your mind and breathe slowly.

- Communicate confidence through your body language. Walk and sit with your shoulders back and your head held up. Look at people when you talk to them and they talk to you. Smile!

- Listen to the questions and don't interrupt. How else will you find out what the selector wants to know? Take your time when you answer.

- Give evidence, evidence and more evidence. Support every claim you make with facts.

- Be honest. Don't make claims about your talents that you cannot support.
- Ask what happens next. How long will you have to wait to hear the selector's decision?

GETTING ON

It has already been mentioned in Part Two that getting on in the voluntary sector generally means that you have to be prepared to move around. Local offices are often small, and their structure tends to be flat. Functions such as finance or research might only be represented by one person, and separate project teams can be small. In this kind of organisation, you may only be able to move one or two steps up the ladder before you get stuck. This also applies in the smaller private sector waste management organisations. Career progress can be made by moving to a larger project with more money and more responsibility, or to a larger office or organisation, with more levels of management.

There are more opportunities for promotion if you are working in the public sector. However, these also tend to be flat organisations based on 'matrix' management structures – where professionals work together on different project teams made up of representatives from functions or other teams. You may start as an officer, move up to senior officer, then go on to being a team leader or project leader before going into management, if that is want you want to do. Each time you move up, you gain more responsibility, accountability, decision-making, people management and administrative duties. As a professional, you may have to think carefully about whether this is what you actually want.

> 'I've always enjoyed my work at the sharp end – getting my teeth into a project and following a design through from the drawing board to completion. The next logical career move is into management, and I feel I'm in a cleft stick, because I don't want to let go of the creative side of the job, but neither do I want to be stuck at this level.'
>
> *Engineer, waste management organisation*

If you enjoy your work as a professional, you may be faced with this dilemma at some stage in your career. The further up you go, the less you are involved with the nuts and bolts of the work, and strategic, tactical and administrative work becomes the focus. Some professionals go on to become very good managers who enjoy their work, but you may have to decide whether to move on, move up or move out.

GETTING OUT

Being your own boss is an attractive idea, and more people in the industry are opting for that route. However, this is not something you can reasonably consider until you have experience and contacts. Starting out and setting up, even with a great deal of experience and a number of contacts, can be difficult, nerve-racking and demotivating. You have to be able to sell yourself and your skills, be very flexible and adaptable, do exactly what the clients want, when they want, and to work all hours, if necessary. Remember, too, that the consultants you actually see are the successful ones, and for every successful consultant, there are likely to be two or three sitting at home watching daytime television or cleaning behind the cooker – and worrying.

'I left my job because I found myself doing more administration and less designing than I wanted to – I had gone for promotion to manager and I wasn't enjoying it. It seemed that fate had intervened, as I had been tentatively approached by a colleague about whether I would consider working on an interesting project for a large organisation on a consultancy basis. So I took the plunge. All did go swimmingly as the project progressed, and I enjoyed it very much. Then, four months later, right on time, the project came to an end. I had assumed that there would be more work where that came from, but the weeks went by and nothing happened. I rang my contact, who told me that there was nothing more planned for that year, but that if there was work, I would get it. They had been very pleased with what I had done for them. Thank you and goodbye.

The next six months were awful. Christmas came and went. The money was running out; I couldn't approach any of the contacts I had made in my former job, as I was contractually bound not to do so; I couldn't claim any kind of state benefit without closing down my business, and the "cold" calls I made were depressing and unproductive. I had decided to apply for a job – any job – when a call came from a colleague in my old office. Was I interested in helping them out with some work? Could I manage to fit it in at such short notice? Could I? Oh yes! After that, things started to get better. More work came in from the first organisation, and I continued to work for the old office. Other work has followed on. Sometimes I'm working like a train – I daren't ever say no! – and sometimes there are gaps of a few weeks. Three years down the line, I know I made the right decision but its been a long haul, with a lot of learning.'

Freelance landscape artist

In the course of our research for this book, we interviewed people at all levels and from all kinds of work in the environment industry. At the end of the interviews, we asked them where they would go if they wanted to get out of the industry. Some of the answers were:

'I wouldn't move out of the industry. I'd move into the private sector: to the "other side", get work as an environmental health officer in a large company, and be better paid.'

Environmental health officer, local government

'Why would I? I've worked hard to get in, and I enjoy it.'

Trust education officer

'I might go back to civil engineering, but I think it would have to be environmentally based.'

Trust project manager

'I'd try for a job abroad with a charity – but I'd stay with environmental science. I could go and work with a large oil company, but even that would have an environmental slant.'

Environmental protection officer

These comments reflect the views of everyone we spoke to. People don't want to get out because their training is in a particular field of environmental science, or because even the jobs they may go for outside the industry are environmentally oriented, or because they enjoy it. There is a fair amount of movement between the various sectors of the industry, but our research showed that once you get in, you don't get out.

Getting out brings you to the end of *The Insider Career Guide to the Environment.*

As we said at the beginning, no book can give you more than a taster of what a particular industry is like. If you still think that caring for the environment is for you, it is now time to start your own research. On the following pages you will find the names and addresses of professional organisations relating to this sector. For details of opportunities with individual organisations, contact your target employers direct or check out their websites.

JARGON BUSTER

If you are planning a career in the environment, it helps to understand some of the common terminology used in this book and environmental 'buzzwords' used within the industry, in environment-oriented literature and in job advertisements. Although this glossary is by no means comprehensive, it will give you brief summaries of frequently used words and phrases.

Agency
Agency is used in this book to mean an NDPB (non-departmental public body) or quango (quasi-autonomous national Government organisation – the term is avoided since it was discredited during the last Tory government). Formerly part of the Civil Service, agencies are set up by the Government as autonomous, not-for-profit organisations with statutory powers in particular fields to manage and enforce the Government's regulations.

Agenda 21
A strategy variously referred to as Local Agenda 21, Rio Agenda 21 or LA21. The result of the 1992 Earth Summit in Rio, which drew up a framework for future action on sustainable development round the world. Described as a 'Local Action Plan for the 21st Century', it has been adopted by the Government to develop new ways of solving problems and working with communities through local authorities, voluntary organisations, community groups and businesses in partnership. It also sets out to promote change in local government which will enable it to work more positively with communities and other organisations.

Central Government
Central Government, Government departments and Government offices are all terms used to describe the organisations in place to direct, control, regulate and administer Government policies. Also known as the Civil Service.

The Civil Service
The Civil Service is used to describe the administrative service of the Government, apart from the armed forces. The DETR is part of the Civil Service, as are the Health and Safety Executive (HSE) and the Employment Service (ES), among others. They administer Central Government policy from offices in all areas of England and Wales.

Civil servant
A civil servant is anyone who works in the Civil Service.

Consultant
An experienced professional whose job is to advise and consult. These people are usually self-employed and are typically contracted by organisations of all kinds to work on a particular project.

DETR
Department of the Environment, Transport and the Regions. The Government department which governs, directs and regulates Government environmental policy.

Environmental health officer (EHO)
Environmental health officers are the officials employed to look after the public's health. The roles of sanitary inspector and public health inspector evolved as the present day environmental health officers. EHOs work impartially and fairly to protect the public from environmental health risks in the areas of: food control; health and safety at work; housing; pollution and environmental protection.

Government initiative
The first step in the process of achieving a specific strategic Government goal or objective.

Local government
A collective term used for local councils and local authorities. These organisations direct, regulate and administer local council policies concerned with matters such as housing, health and safety, food safety, water and air pollution, among others.

New Deal for Communities
The Government's initiative for tackling problems in the community at a local level. It aims to bring together local people, local firms, community and voluntary groups, local authorities and other public bodies to analyse and agree what is to be done and plan how to deliver the results. The initiative targets money on deprived neighbourhoods to improve job prospects, encourage investment in buildings and people and improve neighbourhood management and local services.

Not-for-profit
Not-for-profit or non-profit-making organisations do not make money. Government offices and bodies are examples: these are funded by the Government and are there to provide a service. Charities and trusts rely on voluntary workers and funding from many different sources such as grants available from the European Union and the National Lottery, sponsorships from the business community, and many more.

Private sector
The private sector is a general term used to describe companies and businesses which exist to make a profit.

Public sector
This term is used to describe Central Government offices, local government and NDPBs (non-departmental public bodies or Agencies) – in place to provide a service to the public.

Regeneration
This is the key word in the Government's New Deal for the Community, and is about improving and upgrading communities and places.

Sustainability
Another 'buzzword', described in a DETR Local Agenda 21 Case Study document as follows:

'Sustainability is about protecting the environment, involving people in decisions about it, and sharing out social and economic resources more fairly.'

Urban renewal
A 'buzz' phrase used to refer to the rebuilding and revitalisation of communities and physical environments in the city. Part of the New Deal for Communities, and a more area-specific term for regeneration.

Voluntary sector
The voluntary sector is a general term used to refer to charities and trusts.

WANT TO FIND OUT MORE?

If you are genuinely interested in a career in the environment industry, then you will want to carry out your own research into the areas that appeal to you. Because this is such a diverse industry, there are a lot of organisations you can consult, literature you can access and websites you can visit. Here is a selection of resources to start you off.

Job advertisements
All major newspapers
The Guardian has environmental jobs advertised on Wednesday.

Local press

The Environmental Post
An independent environmental publication which advertises vacancies mainly in conservation, countryside and environmental management sectors.

Environmental magazines, such as *New Scientist, Nature,* the *ENDS Report* (produced by Environmental Data Services), *New Start.*

Newsletters and magazines produced by environmental organisations.

Recruitment agencies
The following agencies specialise in environmental job vacancies:

ADC Environment
PO Box 5903
Basildon
Essex SS12 0YZ
Tel: 01268 468000
www.pathcom.co.uk/ADC

Allen & York
4 Eastbrook House, East Street, Wimborne
Dorset BH21 1DX
Tel: 01202 888986
Fax: 01202 888826
www.allen-york.com/
e-mail: info@allen-york.com

Public interest organisations/ pressure groups/charities

The Sierra Club
85 Second Street
Second Floor
San Francisco, CA
94105-3441
USA
Tel: 00 1 415 977 5500
Fax: 00 1 415 977 5799
www.sierraclub.org/

A non-profit, member-supported, public interest organisation that promotes conservation of the natural environment by influencing public policy decisions: legislative, administrative, legal and electoral.

Greenpeace International
Canonbury Villas,
London N1 2PN
Tel: 0171 865 8100
Fax: 0171 865 8200
www.greenpeace.org.uk/
e-mail: gp-info@uk.greenpeace.org

Earthwatch
680 Mt Auburn St
PO Box 9104
Watertown
Massachusetts 02471
USA
Tel: 00 1 800 776 0188
Fax: 00 1 617 926 8532
e-mail: info@uk.earthwatch.org (UK)

International not-for-profit organisation supporting scientific field research worldwide through its volunteers and scientists.

CPRE – Council for the Protection of Rural England
25 Buckingham Palace Road
London
SW1W 0PP
Tel: 0171 976 6433
www.greenchannel.com/cpre/
e-mail: cpre@gn.apc.org

Funded almost entirely by supporters' subscriptions, donations and legacies. 45,000 existing members who care deeply about England's countryside.

The Green Party
For England and Wales:
1A Waterlow Road
Archway
London N19 5NJ
Tel: 0171 272 4474
Fax: 0171 272 6653
www.greenparty.org.uk
e-mail: office@greenparty.org.uk

Friends of the Earth
Information and Enquiries Unit
26–28 Underwood Street
London
NI 7JQ
Tel: 0171 490 1555
Fax: 0171 490 0881
www.foe.co.uk

The Population Coalition
www.popco.org/

The global population poses the greatest threat to our environment. The Population Coalition has organised a national campaign to educate the wider community at grassroots level.

Earthshare
3400 International Drive NW
Suite 2K
Washington DC 20008
Tel: 00 1 800 875 3863
www.earthshare.org
e-mail: info@earthshare.org

America's leading non-profit making environmental and conservation charity.

The Environment Council
212 High Holborn
London
WCIV 7VW
Tel: 0171 836 2626
Fax: 0171 242 1180

For details, publications and information on careers in the environment.

The National Trust
NT Membership Dept
PO Box 39
Bromley
Kent BR1 3XL
Tel: 0181 315 1111
Fax: 0181 466 6824
www.nationaltrust.org.uk/
e-mail:enquiries@ntrust.org.uk

See the *Yellow Pages* for your local/regional office.

Industrial training and the environment/ institutes and bodies

COSQUEC (Council for Occupational Standards and Qualifications in Environmental Conservation)
Executive Co-ordinator
The Red House
Pillows Green
Staunton
Gloucestershire GL19 3NU

Lantra – National Training Organisation Ltd
Lantra
NAC
Kenilworth
Warwickshire
CV8 2LG
Tel: 01203 696996
www.lantra.co.uk

(Separate regional contacts available for Wales, Northern Ireland and Scotland.)

For enquiries related to all land-based industry training, including agriculture, environmental conservation, fish farming and management, horticulture and tree production and management.

BTCV Enterprises
36 St Mary's Street
Wallingford
Oxfordshire
OX10 0EU
Tel: 01491 839766
Fax: 01491 839646
www.btcv.org.uk/

A limited company owned by the British Trust for Conservation Volunteers, which is the largest organisation in the UK promoting practical conservation work by volunteers. BTCV has worked with a variety of clients to help address industry's growing environmental needs. BTCV Enterprises has a national reputation as a provider of training and government employment training programmes.

Chartered Institute of Environmental Health
Chadwick Court
15 Hatfields
London SE1 8DJ
Tel: 0171 928 6006
Fax: 0171 827 5866
www.cieh.org.uk/

The chartered professional body, independent of local and central Government, set up to promote the principles and practices of environmental health for the benefit of the public. It accredits all courses and training for EHOs. Nearly all EHOs are members of this body. It produces a useful, free information pack.

DETR (Department of the Environment, Transport and the Regions)
Eland House
Bressenden Place
London
SW1E 5DU
Tel: 0171 890 3000
www.detr.gov.uk/

This informative Government department website will give you up-to-date information about policies and initiatives. It also gives information on recruitment. You can send off for an information pack and application forms from them, if you are interested in a career in the Civil Service. Otherwise, ring and ask for this to be sent to you.

The Engineering Council
10 Maltravers Street
London WC2R 3ER
Tel: 0171 240 7891
Fax: 0171 240 7517
www.engc.org.uk/

Institute of Environmental Technology
17419 Sandy Cliff Drive
Houston
Texas 77090
Tel: 00 1 281 440 7665
Fax: 00 1 281 583 9730
www.ela.iet.com./iet.htm

For technical training information.

Institute of Wastes Management
9 Saxon Court
St Peter's Gardens
Northampton NN1 1SX
Tel: 01604 620426
Fax: 01604 621339
e-mail: education@iwm.co.uk

For information on careers in the wastes management industry or details of courses. The Institute is responsible for instigating and awarding professional qualifications and for providing training. It also produces best practice documents and guidelines for the industry, runs an annual conference and exhibition and produces a monthly journal.

The Landscape Institute
6/8 Bernard Mews
London SW11 1QU
Tel: 0171 738 9166

A professional body which sets standards for three landscape professions: landscape architects, landscape managers and landscape scientists. Provides careers information and advice, produces a journal, *Landscape Design*, and operates a reference library for members, which non-members may also consult.

Voluntary Services Overseas
www.oneworld.org/vso/

Government bodies

Environmental Protection Agency
www.epa.gov/

DETR (Department of the Environment, Transport and the Regions)
Eland House
Bressenden Place
London SW1E 5DU
Tel: 0171 890 3000
www.detr.gov.uk/

Countryside Agency
John Dower House
Crescent Place
Cheltenham
Gloucestershire
GL50 3RA
Tel: 01242 521381
Fax: 01242 584270
www.countryside.gov.uk

The United Nations
UN's Earth Summit
www.un.org/

The environmental programme adopted by the United Nations.

UNEP – Home
www.unep.org/

The mission is to provide leadership and encourage partnerships in caring for the environment by inspiring, informing and enabling nations and people to improve their quality of life without compromising that of future generations.

Law and the environment
FreeAdvice's Environmental Law Pages
www.freeadvice.com/

FreeAdvice, rated as the 'leading legal site for consumers', has great, easy to understand information about environmental laws, and links to qualified lawyers nationwide.

Communication
Green Channel Communications Ltd
Crest House
102–104 Church Road
Teddington
Middlesex
TW11 8PY
Tel: 0181 347 6000
Fax: 0181 245 2870
www.greenchannel.com
e-mail: info@greenchannel.com

Provides a global forum and marketplace for commercial, professional and public interest organisations. Promotes positive environmental change through better communication.

Talkway: Talking About the Environment
www.decaf.talkway.com/

Find out everything and talk about the environment. Join Talkway's supercommunity and share your interests with millions of others.

Earth First
South Downs EF
c/o PO Box 2971
Brighton BN2 2TT

Environmental programme information and links.

Planet Peace
Project Peace
PO Box 487
Ashland
Oregon 97520
e-mail: amt@teleport.com

Distributes information regarding environmental causes worldwide.

The Envirolink Network
5808 Forbes Avenue
Second Floor
Pittsburg PA 15217
Tel: 00 1 412 420 6400
Fax: 00 1 412 420 6404
www.envirolink.org
e-mail: support@envirolink.org

Non-profit organisation, uniting volunteers around the world.

The Centre for Conservation Biology: RICE UNIVERSITY
www.conbio.rice.edu/

A central clearing house of conservation biology-related information, resources, university courses and other conservation biology related links, maintained at Rice University under Dr Thornhill, originator of the CCBN.

WANT TO READ ALL ABOUT IT?

www.elibrary.com

Articles with information about the environment at the Electronic Library.

www.barnesandnoble.bfast.com

Listing of books on the environment from Barnes and Noble. Also offers software, magazines, books on tape, author interviews and discussion forums.

The Earth Times
www.earthtimes.org

Daily newspaper on environment, business and current affairs.

E The Environmental Magazine
28 Knight Street
Norwalk, CT 06851
USA
Tel: 00 1 203 854 5559
Fax: 00 1 203 866 0602
www.emagazine.com

Independent news-stand quality publication on environmental issues.

National Geographic Society
Headquarters:
National Geographic Society
1145 17th Street, NW
Washington, DC 20036 4688

New Start
Subscriptions: New Start Publishing Ltd
119 Station Road
Beaconsfield
Bucks HP9 1LG
Tel: 01494 680858
Fax: 01494 681036
e-mail:subs@newstartmag.co.uk

Free weekly magazine which sets out to inform, stimulate and share best practice with everyone working in regeneration and community development. Good for articles, opinions and jobs.

Update
DETR (Department of the Environment, Transport and the Regions)
Eland House
Bressenden Place
London
SW1E 5DU
Tel: 0171 890 3000
www.detr.gov.uk/

A quarterly full colour magazine. Part of the DETR project for information exchange, assisting regional partnerships in the management and delivery of the programmes. For useful information about what's going on.

Waterstones Bookstores
www.waterstones.co.uk

For details of books available.

Careers in the Environment, London Guildhall University, 1995. ISBN: 1 89976 400 3.

Reviews new job opportunities, the qualifications required, what employers want of environmental specialists and further sources of information.

A Career in the Environment, Institute of Biology.

A brief guide covering ecology, environmental protection, waste management, nature conservation, environmental health, planning plus qualifications, follow-up addresses and education and training routes.
   Other titles in this series include:

- *A Career in Agriculture*
- *A Career in Horticulture*
- *A Career in the Natural Resources Industries.*

AGCAS Graduate Careers Information Booklets, Association of Graduate Careers Advisory Services.

A series of booklets on occupations.

Titles include: Agriculture, Horticulture, Forestry and Fisheries, Architecture, Landscape Architecture and Town and Regional Planning, Surveying and Property Management.

Careers in Ecology and Environmental Management, Institute of Ecology and Environmental Management, 2nd edition, 1994.

A booklet outlining environmental career opportunities in many sectors.

Careers in Environmental Conservation, Robert Lamb, Kogan Page, 6th edition, 1995. ISBN: 0 74941 567 3.

Includes up-to-date details of environmental jobs, information on work overseas, types of qualifications and desirable experience and advice on how and where to find openings.

National Rivers Authority, National Rivers Authority, 1992. ISBN: 1 87316 033 X.

National Rivers Authority Facts, National Rivers Authority, 1993. ISBN: 1 87316 008 9.

National Rivers Authority Corporate Plan, National Rivers Authority, 1991. ISBN: 1 87316 005 4.

Law of the National Rivers Authority, William Howarth. University College of Wales, Department of Law, Centre for Law in Rural Areas, 1990. ISBN: 1 87266 200 5.

Careers Working Outdoors, John Humphries & Allan Shepherd, Kogan Page, 7th edition, 1996. ISBN: 0 74941 977 6.

Includes agriculture, horticulture, forestry, environmental conservation, rural crafts and outdoor work in towns and cities.

Courses and Careers in Sustainable Technology: How to Make Green Living Your Living! Allan Shepherd. Centre for Alternative Technology, 1995. ISBN: 1 89804 915 7.

Gives an overview of various environmental career fields, lists of available courses, grants and qualifications plus sources of further information.

Employment and Training Opportunities in the Countryside, Countryside Commission, 1996. Code No. CCP 256.

Seeks to provide an introduction for people planning a career in the countryside. Gives details about employment and training in countryside conservation and recreation.

The Environmental Careers Handbook, Institution of Environmental Sciences, Trotman, 1995. ISBN: 0 85660 188 8.

Outlines career opportunities, gives employer and career profiles, gives advice on choosing a course and getting a job. Also covers general trends in environmental careers.

Working with the Environment, Tim Ryder, Vacation Work Publications, 1996. ISBN: 1 85458 148 1.

Lists opportunities for voluntary and unpaid work in the environment both in the UK and abroad. Also includes advice on choosing this type of work and explains how to go about finding jobs.

Volunteer Work: the Complete Guide to the Voluntary Service, Central Bureau for Educational Visits and Exchanges, 6th edition, 1995. ISBN: 1 89860 104 6.

Advises on volunteer projects worldwide, detailing countries of operation, qualifications and skills required, terms and conditions of work. Includes insights from returned volunteers and advice on development issues, travel and health.

Volunteering for a Better Career, British Trust for Conservation Volunteers, 1996.

An information pack which contains volunteer vacancies, advice on developing a career, useful contacts and comprehensive training brochure.

Working Future? Jobs and the Environment, Tim Jenkins and Duncan McLaren, Friends of the Earth, 1994.

An optimistic discussion paper demonstrating how jobs and wealth can be created by caring for the environment.

Working Out: Work and the Environment, Council for Environmental Education, 1989. ISBN: 0 94761 307 2.

A booklet on choosing a career which will help the environment. Shows how any job can be approached in an environmentally friendly way. Contains case studies and information on ten different areas of employment.

Notes

The Insider Career Guides

Banking and the City
Karen Holmes
ISBN 1 85835 583 4

The Environment
Melanie Allen
ISBN 1 85835 588 5

Information and Communications Technology
Jacquetta Megarry
ISBN 1 85835 593 1

Retailing
Liz Edwards
ISBN 1 85835 578 8

Sport
Robin Hardwick
ISBN 1 85835 573 7

Travel and Tourism
Karen France
ISBN 1 85835 598 2

New titles
Watch out for three new insider guides coming out later in 1999 – the insider guide to successful job search (1 85835 815 9), the insider guide to interviews and other selection methods (1 85835 820 5), and the insider guide to networking (1 85835 825 6).

These and other Industrial Society titles are available from all good bookshops or direct from The Industrial Society on telephone 0870 400 1000 (p&p charges apply).